CHILDREN AND THEIR BOOKS

This edition published by Lector House in 2024

ISBN: 978-93-6138-680-0
Edition copyright © 2024 by Lector House LLP
All rights reserved under the International Copyright Conventions.

Every possible effort has been made to ensure that the information contained in this book is accurate at the time of going to press and the publisher cannot accept responsibility for any errors or omissions, however caused, in this unabridged, slightly corrected republication of the text of the first edition. No responsibility for loss or damage occasioned to any person, acting or refraining from action, as a result of the material in this publication can be accepted by the publisher. The publisher is not associated with any product or vendor mentioned in the book. The contents of this work are intended to further general scientific research, understanding and discussion, only. Readers should consult with a specialist, where appropriate.

No part of this publication may be reproduced, stored in a retrieval system, or transmitted, in any form, or by any means, electronic, mechanical, photocopying or otherwise, without the prior permission of the publisher.

Lector House LLP
Registered Office: H. No. 96, Block C, Tomar Colony,
Burari, Delhi – 110084, India
info@lectorhouse.com
www.lectorhouse.com

CHILDREN AND THEIR BOOKS

JAMES HOSMER PENNIMAN

2024

LECTOR HOUSE
LECTOR HOUSE LLP

CHILDREN AND THEIR BOOKS

BY

JAMES HOSMER PENNIMAN, LITT. D.

Children and their Books

The most vital educational problem will always be how to make the best use of the child's earlier years, not only for the reason that in them many receive their entire school training, but also because, while the power of the child to learn increases with age, his susceptibility to formative influences diminishes, and so rapid is the working of this law that President Eliot thinks that

> "the temperament, physical constitution, mental aptitudes, and moral quality of a boy are all well determined by the time he is 18 years old."

Great waste of the child's time and mental energy in the precious early years is caused by disregard of the way in which his mind unfolds. Not only are children set at work for which they are not yet fitted, but frequently they are kept at occupations which are far below what they might profitably engage in. The child should be guided, not driven; to force his mind is an educational crime. Long continued attention and concentration are injurious, but by using tact a great deal may be accomplished without strain.

At first the aim should be not so much to fill the mind with knowledge as to develop the powers as they are ready for it, and to cultivate the ability to use them. The plasticity of the child's mind is such that a new impression may be erased quickly by a newer one; his character receives a decided bent only through repeated impressions of the same kind. The imaginative faculty is one of the earliest to appear, and a weakness of our educational systems is the failure to realize its importance and to pay sufficient attention to its development. It is well known that imagination is the creative power of the mind which gives life to all work, so that without it Newton would never have found the law of gravitation, nor Columbus have discovered America. The world of make-believe is filled with delight for the small child. He loves stories of imaginary adventure that he can act out in his play,

> "Now with my little gun I crawl
> All in the dark along the wall,
> And follow round the forest track
> Away behind the sofa back.
> I see the others far away,
> As if in fire-lit camp they lay;
> And I, like to an Indian scout,
> Around their party prowled about."

Cultivate his imagination by helping the child to image what he has read. Let us play that we are sailing with Columbus in a little ship over the great green ocean. When we look far off from the top of a wave we see nothing but sky and white-capped water; all around us are angry faces and angry waves.

It is easy to work on the emotions of a little child and thoughtless persons may find it amusing but it is a serious matter, for it has an injurious effect upon his nerves. Ghost stories and books which inspire fear of the supernatural often do much harm to imaginative children.

The boundless curiosity of the child may be aroused and stimulated so that he gets to know himself and the world about him in a way that furnishes him with constant and delightful employment. The growth of his mind is rapid and healthful, because he is reaching out to comprehend and verify and apply to his own purposes the knowledge that he derives from books and that which he obtains from observation. It is not easy to realize the ignorance of children. Dr. G. Stanley Hall found by experiments with a large number of six-year-olds in Boston, that 55 percent did not know that wooden things are made from trees. The world is strange to them; they must grope their way, they are attracted by the bright, the flashy, the sensational, and their tastes will develop in these directions unless they are taught better. Grown-ups estimate in terms of previous experience; the child has had little previous experience to which to refer. Edward Thring says:

"The emptiness of a young boy's mind is often not taken into account, at least emptiness so far as all knowledge in it being of a fragmentary and piecemeal description, nothing complete. It may well happen that an intelligent boy shall be unable to understand a seemingly simple thing, because some bit of knowledge which his instructor takes it for granted he possesses, and probably thinks instinctive, is wanting to fill up the whole."

To impart the desire for knowledge and the power of getting it is next to character-building the most important work of the school. Encourage self-activity to the fullest extent. When the child asks a question be careful not to put him off or discourage him, but if it is possible to show him how to find the answer for himself do so, even at the expense of considerable time and trouble. Aid that quenches curiosity retards mental growth. Many children ask questions merely for the sake of talking, and forget the question before they have heard the answer. As the child gradually becomes able to use them show him how to employ books as tools. Keep reference books on low shelves or tables in convenient places, where it is easy to get at them. Show the child that the dictionary, the atlas, and the encyclopaedia contain stores of knowledge accumulated by the work of many scholars for many years and laboriously classified and arranged for the benefit of seekers after information. Show him how to investigate a subject under several different titles and how to get what he needs from a book by the use of the table of contents, index, and running head lines, and how to use card catalogues and Poole's Index. Help him to look up on the map the places he reads about. Explain the scale of miles and teach him to use his imagination in making the map real; show him that the dots represent towns and cities with churches, parks, and trolley cars, and that the waving lines are rivers on which are steam boats carrying the productions of one section to another.

As he grows older teach him to draw his own conclusions from conflicting statements and to preserve the happy medium between respect for the authority of books and confidence in his own observation. Most boys and girls do not observe and they do not think; they have no opinions except those made for them by others. We are too apt to cultivate the memory and to neglect observation, imagination, and judgment. The result is a wooden type of mind which has too great respect for printed matter and little initiative in accurate observation and in using the imagination and the judgment in making what has been observed and read practically useful.

Encourage the child to talk about what he reads in a natural way, but do not allow him to become a prig by saying what he supposes you would like to have him rather than what he really thinks.

Do not be too eager to stamp your individuality upon the child; he has a right to his own. Find out what his tastes and inclinations are and develop him through them. Ascertain what he is really interested in; very often it is something quite different from what you suppose. His point of view is different from yours. Translate what you wish him to be interested in into terms of his own life and experience. Success in education comes to a great extent from skill in establishing relations between what the child already knows and that which you wish him to acquire.

No part of education has more to do with character-building than the inculcating of a love of good literature. S. S. Laurie calls literature "the most potent of all instruments in the hands of the educator, whether we have regard to intellectual growth or to the moral and religious life". "It is easy," he says, "if only you set about it in the right way, to engage the heart of a child, up to the age of eleven or twelve, on the side of kindliness, generosity, self-sacrifice; and to fill him, if not with ideals of greatness and goodness, at least with the feelings or emotions which enter into these ideals. You thus lay a basis in feeling and emotion on which may be built a truly manly character at a later period—without such a basis you can accomplish nothing ethical, now or at any future time. But when the recipient stage is past, and boys begin to assert themselves, they have a tendency to resist, if not to resent, professedly moral and religious teaching; and this chiefly because it then comes to them or is presented to them in the shape of abstract precept and authoritative dogma. Now, the growing mind of youth is keen after realities, and has no native antagonism to realities merely because they happen to be moral or religious realities. It is the abstract, preceptive, and barren form, and the presumptuous manner in which these are presented that they detest. How, then, at this critical age to present the most vital of all the elements of education, is a supremely important problem. It is my conviction that you can only do so through literature; and the New Testament itself might well be read simply as literature. The words, the phrases, the ideals which literature offers so lavishly, unconsciously stir the mind to lofty motives and the true perception of the meaning of life. We must not, of course, commit the fatal blunder of making a didactic lesson out of what is read. We take care that it is understood and illustrated, and then leave it to have its own effect."

Children behave better when their minds are occupied; an interest in literature has proved in numerous instances to be an aid to discipline in the schoolroom. It is sad to think how little that is refining and elevating comes into the lives of many children. The attitude of the average school boy toward life is shown by the fact that he refers to any stranger as a "guy". The rough horse play of the movies fills such a boy with exquisite delight. To see on the screen a man have a lot of dough slapped in his face is the highest form of humor. His mind is active but it has no suitable nourishment. What is needed is to direct it. President Angell has told us how boys were inspired by that great teacher Alice Freeman Palmer:

"I attended a class in English Literature which she was teaching. The class was composed of boys from fifteen to eighteen years of age, in whom one would perhaps hardly expect much enthusiasm for the great masters of English Literature. But it was soon apparent that she had those boys completely under her control and largely filled with her own enthusiasm. They showed that at their homes they had been carefully and lovingly reading some of the great masterpieces and were ready to discuss them with intelligence and zest."

"Mind grows," says Carlyle, "like a spirit—thought kindling itself at the fire of living thought."

To keep the heart open to elevating influences, to enjoy really beautiful things, to take a dignified and noble view of life, these are the results that must follow association with the best thoughts of the best minds, which is literature. And it is one of the wonders of literature that some of the best of it is adapted to every order of intelligence. When one gets older his mental field widens, he cannot then read all the best, he must choose; but the classic books for children are not so numerous that the child may not read and reread them.

Cultivation of the literary taste of the child may begin as soon as he can talk. He will early take an interest in simple stories and poems and sooner than many suppose, he may be taught to read those which he has already learned by heart. From the beginning reading should be easy and interesting. The child should look forward to it with pleasure. He loves stories, let him see that the best of them are in books told by better story tellers than he can find elsewhere. Help the child to appreciate the book, to take an intelligent interest in it, and gradually lead him up to that love of the best which is the foundation of culture. Do not think that he can see all there is to enjoy at the first reading; a book is classic because it may be read over and over and always show something that was not seen before. There is a distinction which teachers and parents do not always recognize between books, which are beyond the child merely because of the hard words in which the idea is clothed and those in which the thought itself is above his comprehension. "Children possess an unestimated sensibility to whatever is deep or high in imagination or feeling so long as it is simple likewise. It is only the artificial and the complex that bewilder them," said Hawthorne, and because of his knowledge of this fact he wrote his exquisite classics for children. The phraseology of books is frequently different from that to which the child is accustomed. He must be taught to understand thought as expressed in printed words, his vocabulary is limited; in reading aloud he will often pronounce words correctly without any idea of what they mean and far more frequently than you imagine he will receive a wrong impression by confusing words like *zeal* and *seal* of similar sound and totally different meaning. A teacher accidentally found out that her class supposed that the "kid" which railed at the wolf in Aesop's fable was a little boy, and I have had a child tell me that he saw at Rouen the place, where Noah's ark was burned; of course he meant Jeanne d'Arc. "The mastery of words" says Miss Arnold is an essential element in learning to read. Our common mistake is, not that we do such work too well, but that we make it the final aim of the reading lesson, and lead the children to feel that they can read when they are merely able to pronounce the words." "Observation has convinced me" wrote Melvill Dewey "that the reason why so many people are not habitual readers is, in most cases, that they have never really learned to read; and, startling as this may seem, tests will show that many a man who would resent the charge of illiteracy is wholly unable to reproduce the author's thoughts by looking at the printed page."

Children make their first acquaintance with books from the pictures. They like plenty of them with bright colors and broad simple treatment and prefer a rude sketch with action to the finest work of Walter Crane or Kate Greenaway. Illustrations should help the child to understand the story.

Pictures of historic places and objects and adequate reproductions of works of great artists are of value later, for, while the aesthetic sense of the child may be cultivated by surrounding him with the beautiful—flowers, pictures, books, a recognition of the fact that the love of the artistic is of comparatively late development, will prevent much discouragement.

The child learns from his reading what kind of a world he lives in, through books he also becomes acquainted with himself and with his tastes and abilities and sometimes he finds out from them what he is fitted for in life. When carefully directed, reading may be made to cultivate common sense, self-reliance, initiative, enthusiasm, and ability to turn one's mental and physical capital to the best advantage and to make the most of one's opportunities—qualities which ensure success in life, and it also should cultivate the affections and those kindly feelings which make the world a better place to live in. Try to interest the child in books which give true and noble ideas of life where wrong-doing brings its natural consequences without too much preaching. The moral should not be dragged in, the day of the sugar-coated pill in literature is past. The right books are those that teach in a straightforward way that character is better than superficial smartness, that success does not always mean the accumulation of a large amount of money and that it is not a matter of luck but that it depends upon perseverance in faithful work; books which develop the child's sympathies by teaching consideration for the feelings of others, kindness to animals and to all weak and dependent creatures. Lack of reverence is common in the youth of today and books and papers which ridicule old age, filial duty and other things which ought to be respected are all too common. Few have added more to the happiness of mankind than he who has written a classic for children. It takes very unusual qualities to write for them. Sympathy with the child: brightness and simplicity of diction are much rarer than one would suppose until he seeks for them with the child. The first requisite of a book is that it should interest the child, the next is that it should inspire and uplift him. The imparting of information is less important, but whatever information the book contains should be accurate and useful. When a child has learned to appreciate those classics which are suited to his comprehension he will not be likely to waste his time on such futile things as tales of imaginary adventure thickened with a little inaccurate history. He will prefer books which describe what really happened to those which tell what someone writing long after thinks possibly might have happened.

We have a good deal of nervous prostration now-a-days but little refining leisure. Shorter days of labor give more spare time and the schools can render a great service to the nation by teaching how to make the best use of this time and by creating the desire to devote a part of it to the reading of good books and especially to the reading of the American classics. How few resources most persons have in themselves and how flat and unprofitable their lives are. They devote their moments of leisure to killing time, when association with the right reading in early life would have taught them to cultivate that inward eye which has been called the bliss of solitude. He who has a love of reading, however limited his means or however restricted his opportunities may give himself, if he will, a good education. He, who has a taste for good books in youth, will rarely read anything else in maturer years.

"From the total training during childhood" says President Eliot, "there should result in the child a taste for interesting and improving reading, which should direct and inspire its subsequent intellectual life. That schooling which results in this taste for good reading, however, unsystematic or eccentric the schooling may have been, has achieved a main end of elementary education; and that schooling which does not result in implanting this permanent taste has failed. Guided and animated by this impulse to acquire knowledge and exercise his imagination through reading, the individual will continue to educate himself all through life. Without that deep-rooted impulsion he will soon cease to draw on the accumulated wisdom of the past and the new resources of the present, and as he grows older, he will live in a mental atmosphere which is always growing thinner and emptier. Do we not all know many people who seem to live in a mental vacuum—to whom indeed, we have great difficulty in attributing immortality because they apparently have so little life except that of the body? Fifteen minutes a day of good reading would have given any one of this multitude a really human life. The uplifting of the democratic masses depends on this implanting at school of the taste for good reading."

The great men of letters have usually been those who have been accustomed to good books from the mother's knee. Where the taste for reading has not been inherited it must be acquired by continuous effort and some of the world's greatest achievements have been made by men who toiled on in poverty and distress to improve their faculties. There is no fact more uniformly evident in the biographies of great men than that they read great books in youth. Nicolay and Hay say of Abraham Lincoln:—

"When his tasks ended, his studies became the chief pleasure of his life. In all the intervals of his work—in which he never took delight, knowing well enough that he was born for something better than that, he read, wrote, and ciphered incessantly. His reading was naturally limited by his opportunities, for books were among the rarest of luxuries in that region and time. But he read everything he could lay his hands upon, and he was certainly fortunate in the few books of which he became the possessor. It would hardly be possible to select a better handful of classics for a youth in his circumstances than the few volumes he turned with a nightly and daily hand—the Bible, "Aesop's Fables," "Robinson Crusoe," "The Pilgrim's Progress," a history of the United States, and Weem's "Life of Washington". These were the best, and these he read over and over till he knew them almost by heart. But his voracity for anything printed was insatiable. He would sit in the twilight and read a dictionary as long as he could see. He used to go to David Turnham's, the town constable, and devour the "Revised Statutes of Indiana," as boys in our day do the "Three Guardsmen." Of the books he did not own he took voluminous notes, filling his copy-book with choice extracts, and poring over them until they were fixed in his memory. He could not afford to waste paper upon his original compositions. He would sit by the fire at night and cover the wooden shovel with essays and arithmetical exercises, which he would shave off and then begin again. It is touching to think of this great-spirited child, battling year after year against his evil star, wasting his ingenuity upon devices and makeshifts, his high intelligence starving for want of the simple appliances of education, that are now offered gratis to the poorest and most indifferent. He did a man's work from the time he left school; his strength and stature were already far beyond those of ordinary men. He wrought his appointed tasks ungrudgingly, though without enthusiasm; but when his employer's day was over his own began."

Boys like Abraham Lincoln may be relied upon to direct their own reading, but the average child is unable to do this. An important thought which is not always kept in mind by educators is stated thus by Huxley:—"If I am a knave or a fool, teaching me to read and write won't make me less of either one of the other—unless somebody shows me how to put my reading and writing to wise and good purposes." It is not easy to interest in real literature a child whose father reads nothing but newspapers and whose mother derives her intellectual inspiration from novels, but such a child at least lives in a home where there are books, though of an inferior kind, and there is warmth and good lights and leisure to read in quiet and comfort. How different is the case of the poor child, who comes from a tenement where a large family congregate in one room, where the wash is drying, where younger children are playing, there is little light, and no books of any kind. It is with the occupants of such homes that the children's librarian does the most wonderful work. To see a ragged, barefooted child come into a palatial public library, knowing that he has a right to be there and going directly to the shelf choose a book and sit down quietly to enjoy it gives hope for the future of our country. Consider the influence of such a child in his home; he not only interests his brothers and sisters in good books, but also his father and mother. One such child asked a librarian "Will you please start my father on some new fairy tales, he has read all the others." According to the New York Public Library "Reading room books have done more to secure clean hands and orderly ways from persistently dirty and disorderly children than any remedy hitherto tried." There should be enough copies of suitable books and they should be kept on low shelves where the children can have direct access to them. When we spend millions teaching children to read, we should be willing to go to some expense in order to provide them with what is worth reading. It is impossible for those who have not studied the subject to realize the quantity of inane trash with which many children stultify their minds. They read so much that their thought is confused and they cannot even remember the names of the books whose pages are passing before their eyes. The market is flooded with books ranging from the trivial to the harmful which, unless he is properly directed, will divert the child from the real books which he should read and read again. "Ninety children out of one hundred in the public schools below the high school," says Caroline M. Hewins, "read nothing for pleasure beyond stories written in a simple style with no involved sentences. Nine out of the other ten enjoy novels and sometimes poetry and history written for older readers, and can be taught to appreciate other books, but not more than one in a hundred, has a natural love of the best literature and desires without urging to read the great books of the world," and she adds "Stories of the present day in which children die, are cruelly treated, or offer advice to their elders, are not good reading for boys and girls in happy homes."

To form an impression on the white page of the child's mind is a great privilege as well as a grave responsibility. He who makes sin attractive in a child's book or dims the clear-cut distinction between right and wrong will never be able to measure the far-reaching consequences of his work. The child's reading should be constructive rather than destructive. He should learn what to imitate rather than what to avoid, but it is preferable that he should get necessary knowledge of the evil side of human nature from a classic like Oliver Twist than from his own experience or from cheap thrillers. The boy needs to be kept from the vulgar cut-throat story, the girl from the unwholesome romance. Girls should read books that exalt the sweet home virtues. Cheap society stories are not necessarily immoral but they give false ideas of life, warp the mind and encourage selfishness.

The normal boy reads the easiest and most exciting thing that comes to hand, he devours detailed accounts of baseball and football matches and is familiar with the record of every player. The books he reads deal with deeds rather than descriptions. He likes a story that he can act out with not too many characters and with one central figure, he identifies himself with the hero and undergoes in imagination his dangers and triumphs, he likes play with a purpose to it, he is always trying to make something, to accomplish something; he feels unconsciously that he is part of the organic whole of the universe and has work to do. The charm of books like Robinson Crusoe and the Swiss Family Robinson consists in the fact they personify and epitomize the perpetual struggle of mankind with the forces of nature. The boy takes up fads; for a while all his interests are concentrated in boats, then in postage stamps, then in something else. His mind must be occupied, if we cannot fill it with good the bad will get in. Encourage the boy to read books like Tom Brown, or Captains Courageous which show moral worth expressed through physical activity. When he has been interested in the deeds described in such a book have him do something of a similar character to impress the lesson on his mind, for, as Herbert Spencer states:—

"Not by precept, though it be daily heard; not by example, unless it be followed, but only through action, which is often called forth by the relative feeling, can a moral habit be formed," and Edward Thring says:—

"Boys or men become brave, and hardy, and true, not by being told to be so, but by being nurtured in a brave and hardy and true way, surrounded with objects likely to excite these feelings, exercised in a manner calculated to draw them out unconsciously. For all true feeling is unconscious in proportion to its perfection." Building up knowledge without cultivating the power to use it is of small value. Impression should go hand in hand with expression. Knowledge does not become power until you use it. Children should read a great deal and reading should be made attractive to them. The amount of real literature suited to their taste and comprehension is not large and as much as possible of it should be read. Matthew Arnold says that school reading should be copious, well chosen and systematic. There is often a great difference between the books which the child reads when under observation, and those to which he resorts for solace and comfort and turns over and over again when he is alone. The latter are the ones that stamp his character. The school and the public library can never take the place of the home library. It is the books that we own that influence us. The child should know the joy of the ownership of books and there is no better way to interest him in them, than by giving them to him one by one as he reads them. He should have a place where he may keep them in safety and should be taught to respect them and to keep them clean. His books should have all the charm that pretty and durable binding, clear type and bright pictures can give them. When trash is served up in so many alluring forms something must be done to make literature attractive. It is not enough that the child is reading what will do him no harm, his attention should be concentrated on the permanent classics which are suited to his comprehension and taste. He who does not read Aesop and Robinson Crusoe and the Wonder Book in youth will very likely never read them at all. There are a number of books like The Pilgrim's Progress, which are constantly referred to but seldom read. A great deal of the time and mental energy of children is wasted. The total freedom from books and from all other refining influences during vacations is as unnecessary as it is deplorable. An hour a day wisely employed and directed during the summer would give a boy or girl an acquaintance with Longfellow or Hawthorne, that would be a joy and inspiration in all after life. The study of the author's biography in connection with his works has an educational value which nothing else can replace. Consider the influence of a thorough acquaintance with Longfellow or Lowell. The atmosphere which surrounded them, the things that interested them, the sources of their inspiration, the way in which the common experiences of life grew beautiful under the influence of their poetic imagination would be a civilizing force throughout life. That chance is to but a small extent a factor of success, that nothing is attained by the brightest mind without that infinite patience and labor which in itself is genius, the brave way in which such men met trial and adversity:—these are lessons which are not studied as they should be.

Because the imagination is developed early, children are able to find a real delight in poetry even when it is beyond their complete understanding. Sir Walter Scott says:—"There is no harm, but, on the contrary, there is benefit in presenting a child with ideas beyond his easy and immediate comprehension. The difficulties thus offered, if not too great or too frequent, stimulate curiosity and encourage exertion."

As a melody once heard keeps on repeating itself in the ears, so a beautiful thought makes an impression upon the mind that may never be effaced. Charles Eliot Norton says:—

"Poetry is one of the most efficient means of education of the moral sentiment, as well as of the intelligence. It is the source of the best culture. A man may know all science and yet remain uneducated. But let him truly possess himself of the work of any one of the great poets, and no matter what else he may fail to know, he is not without education."

The inspiration and delight derived from familiarity with the best poetry is one of the most precious results of education. The child should be made to understand that school training is but the preparation for the broader education which it is his duty and should be his pleasure to acquire for himself; and to this end it is essential that he be so taught that after leaving school he may look not to the newspaper and the last novel for his ideals, but to the high and worthy thoughts of the classics and especially of the poets of America. Many of the most inspiring deeds of our history have been embodied in poems like Paul Revere's Ride with which every child should be familiar. The works of Longfellow, Whittier, Lowell and Holmes abound in teachings of the highest form of American patriotism and in character studies of the great men who have made our country what it is. The poetry that we have known and loved in childhood has from its very association a strength and sweetness that no other can have. It is to be regretted that children are by no means as familiar with poetry as they should be and that the old-time custom of committing poetry to memory is not more general. Bryant has wisely remarked that "the proper office of poetry in filling the mind with delightful images and awakening the gentler emotions, is not accomplished on a first and rapid perusal, but requires that the words should be dwelt upon until they become in a certain sense our own, and are adopted as the utterance of our own minds." The value of reading poetry aloud is very great. Few school children do it well, and it is especially difficult for them to avoid reading in a sing-song way with a decided pause at the end of every line. "Accuracy of diction," says Ruskin, "means accuracy of sensation, and precision of accent, precision of feeling." Reading poetry aloud is therefore an accomplishment worthy of earnest cultivation. "Of equal honor with him who writes a grand poem is he who reads it grandly," Longfellow has said, and Emerson, "A good reader summons the mighty dead from their tombs and makes them speak to us." To sit still and listen attentively is a polite accomplishment and to reproduce accurately what one has heard is as practically useful as it is unusual.

www.ingramcontent.com/pod-product-compliance
Lightning Source LLC
LaVergne TN
LVHW042046070526
838201LV00078B/820